WHERE'S WALLY?

Based on the
characters created by
MARTIN HANDFORD

THE
ABSOLUTELY
AMAZING

ACTIVITY
BOOK

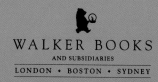

WALKER BOOKS
AND SUBSIDIARIES
LONDON • BOSTON • SYDNEY

GREEN FOREST WOMEN

WELL, HERE WE ARE, WALLY WATCHERS, AT EMERALDA'S BIRTHDAY PARTY. EVERYONE IS ENJOYING THE PARTY EXCEPT ODLAW!

CAN YOU WORK OUT HOW OLD EMERALDA IS TODAY? HERE'S A CLUE:

COUNT THE DOGS WITH THE SPOTS, TAKE AWAY ALL THE DARTS, ADD THE NUMBER OF MUD MEN AND ALSO THE HEARTS.

GOOD LUCK! AND BY THE WAY, EMERALDA IS HOLDING A WHITE HANDKERCHIEF.

DID YOU KNOW?

The pulp of one tree is needed to make 40 copies of a single newspaper.

Natural forest once covered nearly two thirds of the world's land surface, but clearing land for agriculture has reduced this to barely one third.

Trees are among the largest and oldest living things in the world. The tallest tree in the world is growing in Redwood Creek Valley, California, USA. It is 112 metres tall and about 14 metres around its trunk.

A Rocky Mountain Bristlecone tree in the USA is said to be about 5000 years old!

What are the most common trees in your country?
Are any trees in your country very old? Or very tall?
Draw a picture of a forest. Put in lots of trees and hide me in the picture!

THINGS TO DO

These leaves all look the same, but one is slightly different from the rest. Which one is it?

PIRATES

DID YOU KNOW?

Blackbeard the Pirate's real name was Edward Teach.
He used to put burning rope in his beard to terrify his victims.

To avoid a nasty disease called scurvy, English sailors used to eat limes.
The name "limey" is still sometimes used to describe an Englishman!

Some pirates were women. Two of the most terrifying were Ann Bonny and
Mary Read, both of whom plundered the Seven Seas.

Pirates rarely made their prisoners walk the plank. It was far better to put
them to work on the ship.

AHOY THERE,
SHARP-EYED
SHIPMATES. JUST
LOOK AT THIS
CAPTIVATING CREW!
WHILE I HOP ON BOARD AND
PRACTISE MY PIRATING,
THERE'S A LITTLE PROBLEM
WHICH I'D LIKE YOU TO SOLVE.
I'M ON THE LOOK-OUT FOR
A PRICELESS EMERALD RING.
CAN YOU HELP ME FIND IT?
HERE'S A CLUE:

THE PURLOINING PIRATE
HAS A VERY LARGE NOSE,
NO HAIR ON HIS HEAD,
AND NO SHOES FOR HIS TOES.

GOOD LUCK! OH, AND AFTER
YOU'VE GUESSED WHO THE
RING BELONGS TO, HOW
MANY THINGS CAN YOU SPOT
BEGINNING WITH THE
LETTER P?

THINGS TO DO

Try saying these tongue twisters as fast as you can:

Sailing on the seven seas,
sixty salty seadogs saw
some snooty sea serpents.

Making merry maps
for mighty marooned mariners.

Tattooed traitors taking tea,
thieving treasures,
tee hee hee!

Pirate Peg Leg pinched a piece
of priceless plunder.

FLYING CARPETS

DID YOU KNOW?

Persia used to be the name of the country which we now call Iran.

Aladdin, Sinbad and Ali Baba are all characters from some stories called *The Thousand and One* or *The Arabian Nights* which were written in Persia in the fifteenth century.

The greatest King of Persia was Darius. He built a series of roads 2700 kilometres long. Persia could then be crossed by the King's horsemen in one week. It would have been quicker by magic carpet, of course!

Darius's bodyguards were called "The Ten Thousand Immortals" and were expert warriors.

PUZZLE

How well do you know the stories of *The Arabian Nights*?
Subtract the number of Ali Baba's thieves from the number of Arabian Nights.
Then add the number of voyages made by Sinbad. What do you get?

THINGS TO DO

Can you match these shadows to the picture? Look carefully because two of the shadows are the wrong way round!

HEY, WACKY WALLY WATCHERS, JUST LOOK AT THE FANTASTIC FUN THESE FRIENDLY FELLOWS ARE HAVING. THERE CAN ONLY BE ONE EXPLANATION FOR ALL THIS MAGICAL MAYHEM:

THIS IS THE WORK OF A GENIE. OF THAT THERE CAN BE NO DOUBT! BUT YOU'LL HAVE TO LOOK FOR HIM CAREFULLY, AS HE LIVES IN A HOME WITH A SPOUT!

TAKE YOUR TIME AND FIND THE GENIE'S HOUSE. THEN LOOK FOR HIS PET MOUSE. WHITEBEARD SAYS YOU SHOULD BE ABLE TO DO THIS IN LESS THAN A MINUTE, SO GOOD LUCK AND HAPPY HUNTING!

AZTECS

JUMPING JUNGLE JIMMINIES! SO MANY ANIMALS! HOW MANY CAN YOU RECOGNIZE, WISE WALLY WATCHERS? THESE ANIMALS MIGHT BE IN DANGER:

THE AZTECS RAIDED THE JUNGLE, LOOKING FOR SOMETHING QUITE RARE. IT'S BLUE AND WHITE AND IT FLUTTERS, FIND IT AND WARN IT "BEWARE!"

WHEN YOU'VE SOLVED THE RIDDLE, COUNT THE NUMBER OF MONKEYS IN THE PICTURE. THEN TAKE A DEEP BREATH AND SAY "MISCHIEVOUS MADCAP MONKEYS MAKING MAYHEM" AS MANY TIMES AS YOU CAN!

DID YOU KNOW?

There is a wide variety of food and an unchanging climate in the South American rain forest. Because of this there are more birds and they are more brightly coloured than anywhere else on Earth.

The tapir is a relation of the horse and of the rhinoceros. It sleeps during the day and feeds at night.

The pygmy marmoset is the smallest monkey in the world. It grows to only 7 – 10 cm in length!

The loudest monkey in the world is the howler monkey. Its cry can be heard for many kilometres.

The vampire bat is called this because it drinks the blood of sleeping animals! Yuk!

THINGS TO DO

Try and put these pieces of pillar in the right places. Be careful because one of them doesn't fit at all!

UNDERGROUND HUNTERS

HEAVENS! HEAD HONCHO HUNTER REALLY KNOWS HOW TO THROW A PARTY. BUT I CAN'T JOIN IN THE FUN BECAUSE WENDA HAS ASKED ME TO FIND THREE THINGS WHICH SHE HAS LOST:

TWO HATS JUST LIKE WALLY'S ARE WHAT YOU MUST GET. I'VE ALSO LOST SOMETHING TO STOP GETTING WET.

THINGS TO DO

Here is a number code. Each of the letters in the alphabet has been given a number. To find out the name of the person I am thinking about, look at the picture, match the numbers of the things listed below to the letters and then put them in the right order.

1) The number of playing cards with with blue backs.

2) The number of marshmallows.

3) The number of men with moustaches.

4) The number of light bulbs.

5) The number of hunters playing leapfrog.

DID YOU KNOW?

The story of Saint George and the Dragon dates from the third century and is believed to be based on the exploits of a man who lived in Palestine at that time.

A tail-eating dragon is used as a symbol of life in Eastern countries.

The Komodo dragon is not a dragon at all but a huge lizard almost 2 metres long.

The Chinese celebrate the Year of the Dragon. The next Year of the Dragon will be from the year 2000 to 2001.

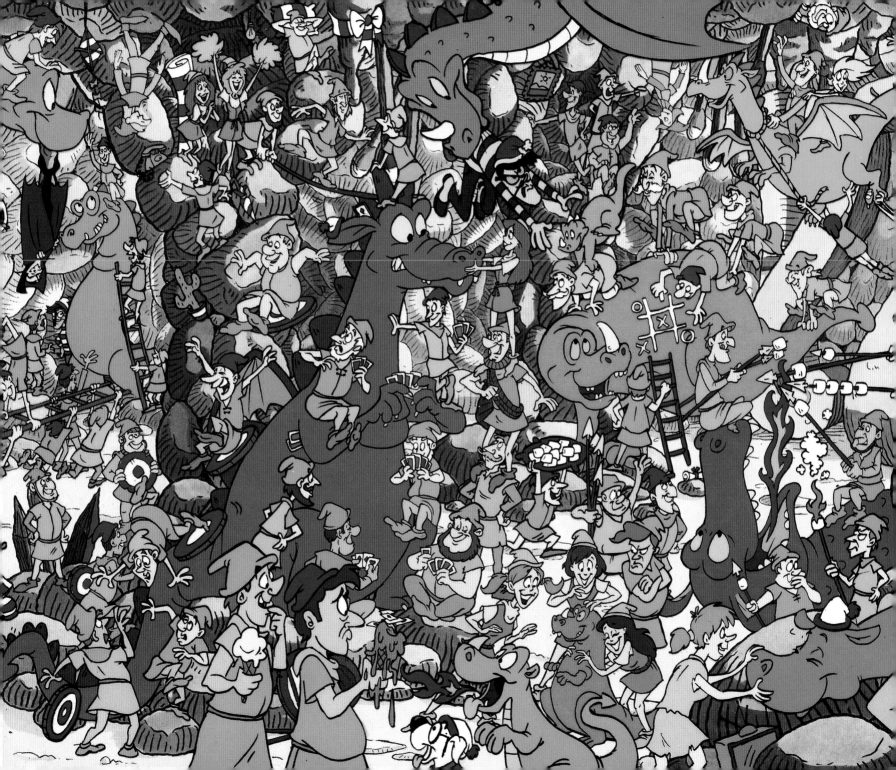

THE GREAT BALL GAME

WHIZZO! WHAT LUCK! HERE WE ARE IN THE LAND OF GAMES ON GRAND CHAMPIONS DAY. JUST LOOK AND SEE HOW FLUSTERED KING FUSSIFUSS IS! HE HAS FORGOTTEN WHERE HE PUT THE TROPHIES TO KEEP THEM SAFE. THEY ARE HIDDEN INSIDE SOMETHING. HELP THE KING FIND THEM BY USING THIS CLUE:

THE LETTERS ARE SCRAMBLED, BUT PLEASE DO YOUR BEST, UNSCRAMBLE THE ANSWER FROM: CURE HEATS REST!

BY THE WAY, FUSSIFUSS IS TO PRESENT TWO TROPHIES. ONE IS FOR JIM THE JUGGLING GENIUS, WHO CAN KEEP FIVE BALLS IN THE AIR AT ONCE, AND THE OTHER IS FOR TWO-AT-A-TIME TIM, WHO CAN PLAY YO-YO AND READ A BOOK AT THE SAME TIME. CAN YOU SPOT THEM?

DID YOU KNOW?

In the sixteenth century, people in the Philippines used yo-yos to knock down animals while hunting.

The Chinese used to fly coloured kites to send messages during battles.

Roller skates were invented in 1759 by Joseph Merlin, a musician, who wanted to skate into a party while playing his violin.

The expression "checkmate" used in chess comes from the Arabic phrase "al shah mat" meaning "the king is dead".

The game of checkers was invented in Egypt in about 2000 BC. Examples of the game have been found in ancient Egyptian tombs.

THINGS TO DO

Look very carefully at the Land of Fussifuss and spot all these objects.

How many different games can you recognize in the Land of Fussifuss?

STONE AGE

WOOF AND I REALLY
LOOK FORWARD TO
SATURDAY NIGHT AT
THE ROCKSY CINEMA.
TONIGHT EVERYONE IS
ROLLING UP TO SEE ROCKBO,
THE LATEST ROCKBUSTER EPIC,
STARRING SYLVESTER STONE.
SOMEONE IS CAUSING MISCHIEF
IN THE AUDIENCE – CAN YOU
SPOT HIM? HE'S THE ONE
HOLDING A MOUSE. HE HAS
HIDDEN SOMETHING FROM GARY
GRANITE, THE CINEMA MANAGER.
CAN YOU SPOT WHAT AND
WHERE IT IS? HERE'S A CLUE:

THE MANAGER'S HUNGRY,
HE NEEDS THIS, POOR FELLOW;
IT CARRIES HIS LUNCH
AND IT'S SMALL,
BLUE AND YELLOW.

WELL, BE AS QUICK AS YOU
CAN – THE ACTION WILL
START AS SOON AS THE SUN
GOES DOWN.

DID YOU KNOW?

The Palaeolithic or Stone Age began about 500,000 years ago!

The dinosaurs had disappeared about 130 million years before the first man arrived!

The Palaeolithic period ended when the Ice Age (about 8000 years ago) changed the climate of the world.

Stone Age man probably first appeared in Africa and Asia.

Ancestors of the American Indians crossed from Asia to Alaska, which were once connected by land.

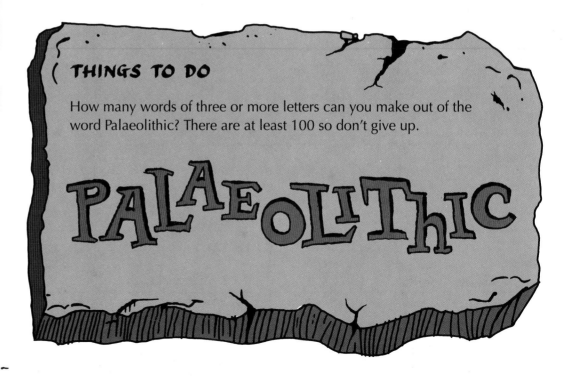

THINGS TO DO

How many words of three or more letters can you make out of the word Palaeolithic? There are at least 100 so don't give up.

PALAEOLITHIC

SPACE AGE

WHEN I CRAVE AN EXTRATERRESTRIAL TREAT, THE LONG JOURNEY TO SPACE CITY IS CERTAINLY WORTH THE SPACESHIP LAG! ON SUCH A VISIT IT'S A SHAME TO HAVE SOMEONE WHO COULD RUIN OUR WONDERFUL DAY. WHO IS IT? HERE'S A CLUE:

SHE'S WEARING STRANGE GLASSES, AND SHOES THAT ARE BLUE. SHE'S LOOKING FOR SOMEONE, I HOPE IT'S NOT YOU!

THERE'S ONLY ONE CREATURE IN THE UNIVERSE WHO CAN EAT MORE HAMBURGERS THAN WOOF. IT'S HUNGRY HORACE SPACE HOG. HE IS WEARING A RED RIBBON AROUND HIS NECK. TO FIND OUT HOW MANY BURGERS HORACE CAN EAT, ADD THE NUMBER OF MILK SHAKES TO THE NUMBER OF ROBOTS.

DID YOU KNOW?

The largest meteorite to have reached Earth landed in Namibia, southern Africa. It weighed nearly 7 tonnes. But before it entered the Earth's atmosphere, it probably weighed nearly 9 tonnes.

Halley's Comet is seen every 76 years or so. Its core is about the size of a city and its tail is millions of kilometres long. It was shown in the Bayeux Tapestry flying over the Battle of Hastings in 1066.

It takes only a few days for a spacecraft to travel to the moon. But to reach Jupiter, 580 million kilometres away, it would take more than a year.

If the distance between the Earth and the Sun were 25 mm, the nearest star would be over 7 km away.

THINGS TO DO

Draw a space creature and a space helmet like this on a piece of thin card.

① FOLD

② PUNCH HOLE

Fold it in half and thread 2 thick rubber bands through the holes as shown.

③ THREAD RUBBER BANDS

④ LOOP

Wind up the rubber bands and then let them unwind at eyelevel. You'll see the creature INSIDE the helmet!

⑤ TWIST

⑥ SPIN!

GRUEL WORLD

WHAT A FEAST OF FUN
THE GRUEL WORLD HAS
COOKED UP FOR US,
WEIGHT-WATCHING
WALLY WANDERERS!
EVERYTHING FROM SAUSAGE-
STEALING AND PIE-PINCHING TO
FRUIT-FILCHING! BUT THE REAL
PROBLEM COMES FROM SOMEONE
WHO LOOKS AS THOUGH HE SHOULD
BE COMPETING IN THE OLYMPICS!
CAN YOU FIND HIM?

THE ARM OF AN ATHLETE –
ARE SPEARS WHAT HE THROWS?
NO, HERE COMES A PIE DISH
TO LAND ON YOUR NOSE!

WELL, THAT SHOULD GIVE YOU
FOOD FOR THOUGHT, WILY
WALLY WATCHERS!

DID YOU KNOW?

Gruel is a thin soup made by boiling oatmeal in water or sometimes in milk! Mmmmm! Tasty!

Popcorn was invented at least 5000 years ago by American Indians. In 1510 Columbus and his men brought popcorn necklaces made by people in the West Indies back to Europe.

The first pies were made in Ancient Greece. They were called "artocreas" or minced-meat pie and they did not have pastry on the top.

You might think that pasta was invented in Italy, but no! It really comes from China. It is supposed to have been brought back to Italy by the Polo brothers – Maffeo, Niccolo and his son Marco, in about 1300 AD.

The word "cereal", which is used to describe any edible grain such as wheat, oats or corn, comes from the name of the Roman goddess of agriculture, Ceres.

THINGS TO DO

Something has gone wrong with these things from Chef Baker Cook's kitchen. Take them apart and put them together again properly. What should they be? Write your answers next to the pictures.

_ _ _ _ _ _ _ _

_ _ _ _ _ _

_ _ _ _ _ _ _ _

_ _ _ & _ _ _ _ _ _

THE LIVING MUSEUM

WOW! WHAT A CRAZY MESS THE LIVING MUSEUM HAS BECOME! WHEN WOOF AND I STROLLED INTO THE WACKY WEST WING THERE WAS CHAOS ALL AROUND. LET'S SEE IF YOU CAN BE A DAZZLING DETECTIVE AND FIND OUT WHO CAUSED THE TROUBLE:

OUT FROM THE PAINTING LIKE MAGIC HE ROSE, WITH MOUTH FULL OF TEETH AND A SWORD ON HIS NOSE!

TO FIND OUT HOW MANY MINUTES WENT BY UNTIL CALM WAS RESTORED, COUNT THE NUMBER OF HATS.

DID YOU KNOW?

The biggest shark ever caught was 6½ metres long and weighed over 3 tonnes.

The oldest museum is the Ashmolean in Oxford, England. It was built in 1683 and was named after the collector Elias Ashmole.

The largest turtle ever found was almost 3 metres in length and weighed nearly 10 tonnes.

The earliest known collector of historical items was King Ashurbanipal of Nineveh, Assyria (668 – 627 BC).

THINGS TO DO

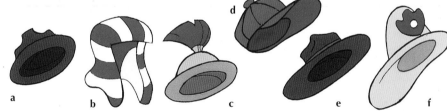

a   b   c   d   e   f

Match the hats to the faces in the Living Museum.
Then draw the funniest hat you can think of for the one face which is left.

1   3   4   5   7
f   c   e
2   6

THE GREAT BALL GAME

- [x] A three o'clock clock
- [x] A television set
- [x] A man with a water pistol
- [x] An iron
- [x] A man wearing roller skates
- [x] A cat chasing a mouse
- [x] A golf club
- [x] 2 footballs
- [x] 5 baseballs
- [ ] 2 blue bowling balls
- [x] A wine glass

GRUEL WORLD

- [ ] 3 mice
- [ ] 4 spoons
- [ ] A fish
- [x] A banana skin
- [x] A boy eating a banana
- [x] A string of sausages
- [x] 3 frothy drinks
- [x] An apple on a fish hook
- [x] A kite
- [x] A man eating spaghetti
- [x] A checked tablecloth
- [x] A man juggling
- [ ] A teapot
- [x] A coffee pot

SPACE AGE

- [x] The Milky Way
- [x] A flying cow
- [x] A jogger
- [x] 3 dogs
- [x] 3 cats
- [x] A spaceman on a pole
- [x] A swimmer
- [x] A giant teddy bear
- [x] A flying cup and saucer
- [x] A police car
- [x] Siamese alien twins
- [x] A space surfboard
- [x] A red bird
- [x] 2 mice
- [x] A space baby and her bottle

STONE AGE

- [x] A striped bag of popcorn
- [x] A snake
- [x] 18 cups
- [x] 2 animals with trunks
- [x] A tray of apples
- [x] A cat and mouse
- [x] 2 drinking straws
- [x] 2 pillows
- [x] A newspaper
- [x] 3 bears
- [x] 2 torches
- [x] A walking stick
- [x] A red and white necklace
- [x] A tug-of-war

THE LIVING MUSEUM

- [x] A fish out of water
- [x] A headless knight
- [ ] A Roman soldier
- [x] A framed king
- [x] A turtle
- [x] 2 grandmothers
- [ ] An upside-down man
- [x] 2 hoses
- [x] 11 firemen
- [x] A pair of binoculars
- [x] A lipstick
- [ ] 2 boy scouts
- [ ] A fire hydrant
- [ ] A telescope

ANSWERS

GREEN FOREST WOMEN

Riddle: 10 dogs with spots; 5 darts; 6 mud men; 2 hearts. Emeralda is 13 years old.
Leaves: Leaf 4 is the odd one out.

PIRATES

Riddle: The ring has been stolen by the big pirate sitting on the side of the ship.

FLYING CARPETS

Riddle: The genie lives in the teapot on the orange carpet, and his mouse is leaning against some boxes on the yellow carpet with red fringing.
Puzzle: 40 thieves subtracted from 1001 Arabian Nights plus 7 voyages = 968.

AZTECS

Riddle: The Aztecs are looking for a butterfly. It is on the right of the picture, next to the Aztec who is pretending to be a monkey.
There are 13 monkeys in the picture.
Pillar: A = 2; B = 5; C = 1; E = 3; F = 4. D doesn't fit at all.

UNDERGROUND HUNTERS

Riddle: Wenda's hats are both being worn by dragons. Her umbrella is between the rocks in the top left corner of the picture.
Number code: The name you should have found is WENDA.
There are: 14 playing cards with blue backs; 23 marshmallows; 5 men with moustaches; 1 lightbulb; 4 hunters playing leap frog.

THE GREAT BALL GAME

Riddle: King Fussifuss hid the trophies inside a TREASURE CHEST. Jim the Juggling Genius is sitting on the roof. Two-at-a-time Tim is sitting on a giant baseball.

STONE AGE

Sylvester Stone is on the left of the entrance to the cinema.
Riddle: He has hidden the manager's lunch box next to the woolly mammoth.

SPACE AGE

Riddle: She is in the bottom left-hand corner of the picture.
Hungry Horace Space Hog can eat 10 burgers in one sitting: 3 milk shakes plus 7 robots.

GRUEL WORLD

Riddle: The pie-thrower is standing in front of the giant teapot.
Puzzle: Chef Baker Cook's mixed-up items are: saucepan; teapot; colander; cup and saucer.

THE LIVING MUSEUM

Riddle: The trouble was caused by the swordfish in the picture frame. 22 minutes went by before the museum calmed down.
Hats: The hats and heads go together like this:
a = 6; b = 5; c = 3; d = 7; e = 4; f = 1.

MORE THINGS TO DO

The fun's not over yet Wally watchers! Have a look at the back cover. Each of the characters there appears more than once in our book. Can you spot them all, and find 12 scrolls?

The "creature" below is made up of 1 element from each of the large pictures in this book. Can you find which picture each piece comes from?

Happy hunting!

First published 1993 by Walker Books Ltd
87 Vauxhall Walk, London SE11 5HJ

7 8 9 10

Text © 1993 Martin Handford

The right of Martin Handford to be identified as author of this work has been asserted by him in accordance with the Copyright, Designs and Patents Act 1988.

This book has been typeset in Optima.

Printed in Great Britain

British Library Cataloguing in Publication Data
A catalogue record for this book is available from the British Library.

ISBN 0-7445-3241-8